MONTENEGRO

Komovi, 2478 m

*"I wonder the sun how can it
set, when nowhere can such
beauty be met!"*
Ljuba Nenadović

*Montenegro is the first
and for the time
being the only
ecological country
in the world.*

WELCOME AMONG ITS BEAUTIES!

A small but unique country of the central Mediterranean was declared ecological country in 1991.

There are few countries in the world that along their borders, as if skillfully lassoed, occupy an area of 13.812 square kilometers and possess 293 km of unique coastline, called "pearl-like" by the local people, and around 70 mountain peaks over 2000 m high not less attractive and challenging by their beauty as it is case with Montenegro (with borderline of 614 km).

That country truly exists! It is called Montenegro.

The intensive connection of the coastal and mountain regions of Montenegro cannot be feasible in other parts of the Mediterranean. This is mostly conditioned by the "games of nature" that created the alpine forests with the features of that mountain type, out of the sea and all that on very short distances. The abundance of conifer forests intersected by canyons-recorders of beautiful haymaking, snow blankets and "capitals"- representatives in flora and fauna, of clear, fast rivers and perfectly clear lakes and fresh mountain air is a true privilege to tourists who can get from warm Montenegrin coast to the coldest mountain regions of the

 Biogradsko lake

north, in only two-three hours, using this guide. The length of its land borders with the neighboring countries is 614km, with Serbia 203km, with Albania 172km, with Bosnia & Herzegovina 225km, and with Croatia 14km. This small country, fine not only in the mentality of its people but also in its intact nature has a wide pass on the Adriatic Sea along its southwest. The seacoast length almost equals half its continental borders length (293 km). There is around 200 km airline distance between two most distant parts of Montenegro. The geographical centre of Montenegro lies in the area of the Morača River spring and except its south part, Ulcinj coast, its other parts don´t exceed 90 km distance from it.

AT THE CROSSROADS OF THE WORLD

The relief of Montenegro is all in the dynamic of its contrasts, cruel and dramatic and, at the same time, calm and filled with the light of the sunny sides. Like the guardians, many of its hills and rocks, canyons and roads represent the remains from the mythological times.

It particularly refers to former settlements and crossroads full of hints and living testimonies about the cultures and civilizations from the oldest times. The most important archeological find is Red Cave near Nikšić. The objects found there suggest the existence of life even in the oldest prehistoric times. The other interesting finds are Gotovuša near Pljevlja and Beran-krš near Berane.

The Illyrians are supposed to have been the first inhabitants of Montenegro.

Today, former Illyrian towns that represent the rich finds are great attraction to archeolo-

gists from all over the world. Hollow axes found in the finds Budimlja near Berane and in Smrduša near Nikšić led scientists to conclusion that **Aegean migration** had been running over the territory of present Montenegro.

In the 2nd century BC the Illyrians were conquered by the Romans and according to the writings of the old spies they wore grapevine beside their sword coverings and felt more and more insecure as they were getting further from warm sea to the north. The famous reinforced Roman roads remained after them, of which the most famous was from Cavtat via Budva to Skadar and Drač where it attached to well-known road called Via Egnatia. The newly conquered territory was then added to the Province of Dalmatia. The most important monument from that time is the town of Doclea founded in the time of Tsar Flavio. Its ramparts haven´t been studied enough due to incomplete historical-artistic reconstruction, and due to some uncontrolled and unskilled excavations done at the end of the 19th century, it may not be possible at all. At the end of the 3rd century, Tsar Dioklecijan separated new province called Prevalitania from the territory of Dalmatia.Its borderline extended from Budva, in the south, to the mouth of the Lim River in the Drina River, in the north. After the administrative separation of the Empire in 395, it was also the borderline between the East and West Roman Empire. There are still ramparts of the Roman towns - Medun in the village of Kuči and Municipium near Pljevlja as many others, particularly those in the coastal area that are irreplaceable testimony of pre-Slavic, Roman civilization and culture.

There are the preserved traces of the earliest Christian art that is supposed to have started developing on the Adriatic coast between the 3rd and 4th century. A remainder of that art is a floor mosaic with motives of the vine leaf and of crossed bread slices, a symbol of communion, found in a villa in Mirište in Petrovac on the sea. The Slavs' migrations started at the beginning of the 7th century.

In the territory of present Montenegro they founded their first principality around the Roman town of Doclea and it kept the name Doclea up to the end of the 10th century when it got a new one- Zeta in the 11th century. The official writing type was Cyrillic and they used the old Slavic language.

"Chronicle of the priest of Doclea" is one of the oldest written monuments in the Slavic South. Some of the stories from this chronicle excited the imagination of the people at the later times, particularly "Hagiography of Vladimir". Love story between the Duke of Doclea, Vladimir and the daughter of Macedonian Tsar Samuilo, Kosara, Vladimir`s nobility, his capture and taking to the dungeon by an act of fraud, inspired different authors to create their works later. Culture development was greatly influenced by Greece and Byzantium. Many Slavic churches were built in the area of Skadar Lake and its islands and along its shore. The remains of the church of Prečista Krajina (Ostros, Skadar Lake shore) and St. Triphon`s Cathedral (Kotor, 809) are from the earliest period. The foundations of the independent country of Zeta were laid in the 9th century. When Michael got the rank of Rex Sclavorum from the Pope Grgur VII, Zeta was recognized as a kingdom.

After the schism in 1054, different civilizations started dramatic struggle for dominance over this territory changing their homes fast and easily in the way the warriors` blood throbs against their temples. Going through many changes, either as an independent or as

In the territory of Montenegro there are 2.800 different plant species and subspecies, and even 22 species that cannot be found in other parts of the world.

a country fallen into someone`s power, this country continued to exist and develop up to the end of the 15th century. There is a lead seal of Peter, the ruler of Doclea preserved with an inscription written in Greek **"Peter, Archonte of Doclea, Amine"** on it.

The Bishopric of Bar was founded in 1089. At the beginning of the 12th century, the country of Zeta divided into many pieces due to the internal struggles over "the right on the seal" leaving the state territory to Stefan Nemanja, the great head of the tribal state that attached it to the territory of Raška. After Tsar Dušan`s death, in the middle of the 14th century, the country of Zeta became united and regained its independence but not for too long. When the Serbian domain first fell into Turkish control in 1439, the territory of Zeta started being greatly influenced by Venice whose dominance had already been strengthened in the coastal region. The rulers of Gornja Zeta -Crnojevići acknowledged the supreme control of the Republic of Venice.

Like many other periods, this one was also depicted in one of the national poems called **"Wedding of Maxim Crnojević"**.

These national songs created while the Montenegrins would sit at night by the fire playing their national instrument `gusle` and singing, passed from generation to generation and became the irreplaceable illustration of historical happenings and memories of these people.

When war between Turkey and Venice came to terms, Ivan Crnojević decided to move his residence from Žabljak to Cetinje in 1452.

At the beginning of the 15th century, the Ottoman Empire decided to attach Montenegro to Skadar Sanjak. The following 400 years of Turkish dominance characterize constant Montenegrins` struggle for their freedom.

The name of Montenegro was first mentioned in the middle of the 14th century. It was probably named after the "black" forests that covered most part of Lovćen and of old-Montenegrin mountains area in the Middle Ages.

First information about Montenegro`s population dates from 1552. **Danilo I**, the founder of Petrović dynasty was declared a bishop in 1697. The slogan "struggle for freedom" was the imperative of his reign.

Petar I Petrović (ruled from 1784 to 1830) managed to defeat the Turkish army through very difficult and bloody struggles, and thanks to the strength of his character he brought in some important educational changes in the society, he strived and achieved to unite and reconcile Montenegrins` tribes and tribes from the Hills strengthening the country in that way.

He is the author of the work of great cultural-historical importance called "Epistles" that remained as a spiritual trace and a warning to the future Montenegrins. That work also represents a special treasure of national spirit, customs and beliefs of that time.

Petar II Petrović- Njegoš (1830-1851) was a poet, a bishop and a ruler at the same time. After the agreement with Austria, he managed to get the recognition of the Montenegrin borders. This quite unusual ruler also managed to found the first culture institutions in the new country.The most amazing and astonishing thing when he is concerned is the difference between the things he achieved as an artist, a poet and the life circumstances he lived in.

Sea bottom detail

Large Šiško Lake is situated on Bjelasica at an altitude of 1.660m, with the surface of 29.080m² and its highest depth of 3,2m. Small Šiško Lake is 1 km away with the surface of 8.500m².

On one side, there were hardly 30 boys who were trying to learn reading and writing skills in the newly founded, first Elementary school (1834) while on the other side, Njegoš created his masterpieces, on which the society with the most progressive material and spiritual culture could only envy. **During the reign of Danilo Petrović in 1852, Montenegro was declared a principality** (it included Cetinje, Katunska nahija, Bjelopavlićka valley and part of the Hills).

According to the register from 2011, Montenegro had the population of 620.029 inhabitants.

Capital: PODGORICA

Old Royal Capital: CETINJE

Nationality- Montenegrins 43%, Serbs 32%, Bosnians 9%, Albanians 7%, Muslims 5%, Croats 1%.

There are 1.256 settlements in Montenegro.

Climate in Montenegro is very complex and varies from the Mediterranean in the south to the severe mountain in the north.

The average temperature in July is 27,1°C in Podgorica and 14,5°C on Žabljak. The width of the sea surface is 12 nautical miles (22.224 m). Total surface of the sea (with the coast length of 293 km) is about 4.800 square kilometers.

In his scientific works, Jacque Cousteau, recently passed away and unsurpassable explorer of the sea mentioned the Adriatic Sea as one of the cleanest in Europe. In front of the Bay of Boka the Adriatic is the deepest (1330 m) while it is the widest between Bar and Brindizi (211 km or 114 nm). This is also the zone of the greatest saltiness of 38%, the zone where the

The length of bathing season in Montenegro a month longer than it is in Malaga, Spain or Nice, France or even two months longer than in Sevastopol, the Black Sea

sea is the most transparent (69 m) and of the warmest water (on average 25°C in July). There are 2.720 sunny hours a year in this part of the Montenegrin coast, which classifies it among the sunniest of the Mediterranean, but, at the same time, on the slopes of the Orjen mountain, in the area of Krivošije, in the locality called Crkvice at an altitude of 1.097m there is a meteorological station with precipitation of 5.155 mm/m^2 and with absolute daily record of 480 mm/m^2 (recorded on 21 November 1927). This record can be found in only one more place called Karapandza under the Himalayas, opposite of Bengal Bay.

The annual temperature of the coastal seawater is 17,4°C. On average there are 7,2 sunny hours and average annual air temperature is above 17°C. These values make the length of bathing season in Montenegro a month longer than it is in Malaga, Spain or Nice, France or even two months longer than in Sevastopol, the Black Sea.

Underwater fishing is also possible along the Montenegrin coast due to alternating changes of the shallow and deeper seawater. The central and south part of Montenegrin coast (between Bar and Ulcinj) is the zone of the most beautiful beaches on the Adriatic.

Among them the largest is Velika plaža in Ulcinj (12,5 km long with average shore width of 70m, with shallow waters of around 100m and the capacity of 100.000 swimmers), ideal for children and non-swimmers. Near these beaches or in their direct vicinity, many tourist and hotel towns have been built, such as Budva, Bečići, Petrovac, Sutomore, Velika plaža and Ada Bojana that is placed along Montenegrin-Albanian border.

Montenegro is rich in lakes.

The largest one is Skadar Lake, then Šasko Lake and Plavsko Lake. The deepest one is Black Lake on the Durmitor (49m).

The largest glacial lake is Pivsko Lake.

There are 29 glacier mountain lakes in Montenegro, of which Plavsko lake is the largest. Hydrographic system of Montenegro consists of two basins - the Adriatic (47,8%) and the Black Sea (52,2%).

The largest rivers in Montenegro are - the Tara, the Ćehotina, the Piva, the Lim, the Zeta and the Morača.They are very rich in fish.

The most interesting fish in the rivers of Montenegro are mountain trout, chub, lipljen, pike.

The most common fish in Skadar Lake are bleak, eel and carp.

The Adriatic Sea is rich in different high-quality fish as well as in exotic sea fruits that are specialties of local fish restaurants on the shore.

Ostrog Monastery

THE
COASTLINE

*"I wonder the sun how can it set
when nowhere can such beauty be met."*

The truth expressed through these lines by **Ljuba Nenadović** will be confirmed to all tourists as soon as they see the unique colours of the Bay of **Boka**, the bay placed between the highest coastal mountains - Orjen (1875m) and Lovćen (1749m). 105,7 km long and winding coast resembles a necklace made of red roofs of the old stone palaces, where from the sounds of seagulls and bell ringing echo and that are eternally reflected in washed by rain squares, of the markets called "pjaceta" and of the piers with boats filled with fishnets.

The peace of the purple blue sea, from Herceg Novi, Bijela, Kamenari, Risan, Perast, Kotor, Prčanj via Verige to Lepetani and Tivat, united with lime and granite mountain colours creates the unique spectrum that is recommended by oculists to those who have eye problems.

*Rose - this used to be the shelter for sailing boats but today it is a small fishing place.
It is about 3 kilometers away from Herceg Novi.*

"Here everything lives of the sun, because of the sun, for the sun."
Zulfikar Dzumhur visiting Herceg -Novi

Clock Tower was built by master Mustafa, and on the request of Sultan Mahmud, in1667. It was the main town entrance for a long time.

Herceg Novi

Rafailovići

*The island of Mamula - During the Venetians dominance it was called Rondoni and its current
name it got in the 19th century after an Austro-Hungarian called Lazar Mamuli. During the First and
Second World War there used to be a prison. It is situated at the very entrance of the Boka Kotorska Bay,
3,4 miles away from Herceg-Novi.*

The island of Mamula

Boka kotorska. Due to its natural features (a passage between Cape Oštra and Cape Arza of 2.950m width and Verige strait of only 340m), the Bay of Boka is one of the safest bays in the world, which in the oldest times conditioned the development of maritime economy and science on its coast, particularly in Risan and Kotor, and more earlier, even the development of architecture.

One of the first cathedrals, older than many other church temples in the world, was built in Kotor. The building of the Cathedral of St. Tryphon started in the 9th century after the arrival of the Slavs, and ended in 1166. It is 544 years older than the Church of St. Paul in London, 460 years than the Basilica of St. Peter in Rome, 313 years than the Temple of Assump-

Not far from Risan, there is a settlement called Lipci famous for its prehistoric drawings made on a rock that suggest the existence of life in Boka around 3.000 BC.

tion in Moscow, 69 years than the Notre Dame in Paris and 169 years older than the Visoki Dečani.

This well-preserved and monumental building is famous for its low-relief plastic, old valuable frescoes and ciborium. Material culture of Boka is rich in Roman mosaics found in Risan, in museums and galleries with ancient archive documents and in masterpieces of the old artists. Two islands that are also two tourist settlements, St. Marco`s island and the Island of Flowers, look like two green pillows that invite tourist to take a rest, have fun and recreate on the peaceful blue bed of the bay.

The Bokellian Navy was formed in the territory of the Bay of Kotor in the 12th century, when Kotor was ruled by Nemanjić dynasty. It consisted of the following ships- Perast,

Kotor, Prčanj and Dobrota. This "the oldest society" made the written Statute in 1436 that is also kept today. In the history of this area there are many seamen who sailed different seas and oceans. That experience has been transferred to the younger generations and it is now a part of their tradition.

The Russian soldiers used to study naval skills in the school of captain Marko Martinović. A man from Boka called Matija Zmajević, the famous seaman served the Russian Queen Catherine the Great. He was decorated with an order of "Alexander Nevski" for his special merits (the victory at Ganguta as a member of Baltic Navy) and he also got the admiral`s rank in Russian Navy. The blue admiral`s flag of Baltic Navy is kept in Perast. Zmajević was buried with full hon-

The Italian saint Lepopold Padovansk was born in Herceg-Novi.

ors in Moscow in 1735. Unfortunately, his palace in Perast, dating from 1670 and known for philosophical inscriptions on its stone windowpanes that face the sea is all in ruins now.

Ivan Visin, a citizen of Prčanj (thanks to his accomplishments) joined this great man from Perast as he succeeded to sail around the world by his sailboat for seven years, in the period between 1852 and 1859.

In that unique and "unsaid" Bay of Boka, a tourist can satisfy all his desires no matter if it is a total rest, recreation, hospital-therapeutic care or different cultural- historical research in the area of the old civilizations or in undiscovered underwater life.

Herceg Novi.
"Here everything lives of the sun, because of the sun, for the sun"

The Illyrians were the first who enjoyed the benefits of this sun, and since the 5th century BC that were the Greeks. The Roman Empire had dominated this region in the 2nd century up to 476 when the area of Herceg Novi fell under the Byzantium control.

In September 1382, the Bosnian King Tvrtko built the first fortress along the very seashore and since then present-day Herceg Novi started its development. King Tvrtko called the town Saint Stephen, while its current name it got after Herceg Stjepan who, in 1449, built the second fabric factory in Europe but the first in this territory. Herceg Novi, the exotic outdoors garden represents the shelter for the particular, choosy tourist clients all over the year thanks to **Igalo Spa** and its record mild climate in the Adriatic as well as to its well-known **"Mimosa Celebration"** that is held in February.

"When the pearls of nature were sown, on this soil an overflowing handful was gathered."
Lord George Gordon Byron on the Boka Bay

During its history Herceg Novi was dominated by different conquerors (the Venetians, Turks, French, Austro-Hungarians, Russians and even the Spanish). The remainder of Spanish dominance is the fortress above the town called " Šparjola". The very important documents of the material and spiritual culture are kept in the Archive and National Museum of Herceg Novi. In the recent history, there has been a summer residence of the President of SFRJ, Josip Broz- Tito situated in Igalo.

Igalo is situated on north-west coast of Topla bay. Sea bottom around Igalo is covered with the sand and curative mud which is used for curation of rheumatic.

Kumbor - port in Boka Kotorska. Roadstead in front of Kumbor is the best in Herceg Novi`s bay. In the XII century, the Turks had fortification Vrbanj in Kumbor, which was defending Herceg Novi; it was occupied and destroyed by people from Perast.

Bijela is situated on the northern coast of Tivat bay. Its today's name - BIJELA was mentioned in Czar Dusan's Charters in 1351. From that period, altar`s frescos in an old church dedicated to Ascenesion of Madonna. It was preserved and merged with new church dating from 1824.The book "Oktoih", printed in 1493, is kept here.

Opposite Perast, a town of captains, there are two islets, Our Lady of the Rock and St. George` s famous for their beauty and historical value.

Name "Gospa od Škrpjela" have 126 ships in Boka Kotorska. Perastum was a name of the city mentioned in 1326. Turks had never occupied it, even the whole north Boka was under their reign.

 Tivat

Risan as Illirian settlement was for the first time mentioned in the 229 BC. Saracens attacked it in 865, and Czar Samuil attacked it too in 976. From the X century it was part of Principality Travunja, later on was under the reign of Balsic family. From 1397 it was under the reign of Stjepan Tvrtko I, and from 1451 under the reign of Republic of Dubrovnik. Turks keeps it under their reign from 1539 to 1687, and later on it shares destiny of all other places in Boka Kotorska.

In 1326, Kotor gets its first pharmacy store. In 1350 Kotor gets its first hospital. Pharmacists and doctors were mostly Italians, elected by Big Council of municipality on George's day.

Kotor is situated on the south-east part of Kotor bay under the Lovcen mountain.

The old part of the city was developed at little triangular space, surrounded by city's wall reaching the fortress of St. Ivan (260 m). Kotor is surrounded by walls - almost 5 km long, 20 m high, and 2-15 m wide. There are two walls and both of them end near fortress St. Ivan. From the city to fortress there are 1 426 stairs.

Perast - In 1698, the Russian Tsar, Peter the Great sent 70 his residents of a boarding school to get proper education in this small coastal place, which tells that Naval School of Perast was famous around the world. A master of his trade Marko Martinović (1663-1716) ran this school. Many seamen from Perast were the admirals of the Russian Navy and what is also interesting is the fact that Perast never fell under the Turks' control that proves a cannon placed in Visković Palace. In terms of architecture, Bujović Palace is standing out. Today, it houses the Town Museum of Perast. It was built according to the project of the Venetian architect Giovanni Battista Fonte in 1694.

The narrowest street in the world resides in Kotor, and it is called "Let me pass". The street is so narrow that two men barely can pass by each other.

Since the 9th century, the seamen of Kotor visited all known ports of that time sailing by their boats.

Kotor was found in the 4th and 5th century AD under the supreme government of Byzantium and under the name of Catarum. It got its current Slavic name in the 9th century. Kotor fought against Turkey and Napoleon`s France for a long time, then supported by Russia and Montenegro it got its freedom and then the Austro-Hungarians occupied it from 1814 to 1914.

Tivat was first mentioned in 1326. This is the town where from, on 1 February 1326, inspired by October revolution and involving all the shipping in the Bay of Boka started the rebellion of the ship St George`s mariners, one of 40 ships anchored in the Bay of Tivat.

Beside its accommodation capacity, there are two significant advantages for tourism of Montenegro that Tivat possesses - modern airport and important function of yachting tourism in future.

Today, Kotor is trade, industrial, culture, educational and tourist center. Modern tourist services are provided to tourists who come to Kotor to enjoy the beauties of the Bay of Boka Kotorska, its mountain massifs and culture-historical heritage.

OUR LADY OF THE ROCKS -THE JEWEL OF BOKA

The little town of Perast, a treasure trove of valuable works of the cultural, historical, and artistic heritage of Boka, is nestled in one of the most beautiful areas of Boka Kotorska, at the base of the hill of St. Elias. Its valuable monuments, churches, chapels, slender bell-towers, the City Museum, exquisite palaces, balconies and coats of arms have all been well-preserved.

During the winter, it is protected from the northern winds, turned towards the sun and the sea, while a comfortable breeze from Verige helps cool down the town during the heat of the summer.

Two picturesque islets stand guard before it. The natural islet of St. George houses a 17th century church of the same name, as well as the Perast cemetery, dating from 1886, and an ancient Benedictine abbey, from the 12th century.

This secretive islet, over-grown with dense vegetation and slender cypress trees could have, perhaps, served as the inspiration for the painting. The Island of the Dead by Swiss painted Böcklin. Not far away from it, lies the man-made islet, Our Lady of the Rocks, with a sailors' votive shrine by the same name. The islet was built by constant heaping up of the stones that started in the middle of the 15th century , on the 22nd of July, 1452, to be more exact, and has been going on, to some extent, to this day. The islet covers an area of 3030 m^2.

According to tradition, the painting of Our Lady in Perast becomes known in 1452.

The building of the church on the rock is connected in this tradition with one of the Mortešić brothers' recovery from illness. They kept the painting in their house, after they found it one night, while out fishing, in the middle of the sea.

To show their appreciation for the miraculous recovery, they took the painting to the church of St. Nicolas. It was later decided to build a church on the rock near the islet of St.Elias, to honor Our Lady and house this painting.

It is believed that the main altar of the shrine is situated on the very reef where the painting was found. Since the word škrpion is known to Croatian fishermen and sailors as referring to a see reef or rock, the name Our Lady of Škrpjel, then, means Our Lady of the Rocks-a befitting name for shrine built upon one.

The church is rather small and simply built of fine stone from the island of Korčula. It is comprised of a navel and a chapel (an apse), covered with a dome.

Light enters the church through two oval windows. The building was done by master builders Vuk Kandijot and Petar Dubrovčanin.

The interior of the church is an extravagant picture gallery. Sixty eight oil-on-canvass paintings, hang on the side walls and the ceiling. The ceiling is painted with scenes from the lives of Mary and Christ, as well as images of evengelists and church elders.

The creators of this valuable collection in the church of Our Lady of the Rocks are the Archbishop of Bar, Andrija Zmajević, and Tripo Kokolja, a painter from Perast.

Our Lady of the Rock *is an artificial island created by piling up stones around an existing rock where was, according to the legend, found an icon of the Holy Mother of God and later on, in 1630, the sailors decided to erect the Testament church dedicated to Our Lady Of the Rock on the surface of 3030 m². The interior of the church is decorated with 68 paintings of the Baroque master Tripo Kokolja and the dominating icon, 10m long is called "The Tear of the Virgin Mary".*

The impressive ceiling of the church of Our Lady, covered in paintings of Tripo Kukolja

St. Tryphon`s Cathedral

is the most significant medieval monument in Kotor. It was erected and consecrated in 1166 on an earlier holy place where a small pre-Romanesque church, dedicated to the same saint, had been built at the beginning of the 9th century. It was being built in the Romanesque style with the central nave (out of three) twice as wide as the two aisles and the naves ending in semicircular apses. Two bell towers adjoin the west facade interconnected by arched doorway. The catastrophic earthquakes in the 16th century had seriously damaged the cathedral. In the reconstruction that took place between 1584 and 1613, its interior got a new Renaissance-Baroque appearance. In the earthquake in 1667, the Romanesque bell towers were destroyed and reconstructed later in the Baroque style together with the west part of the building. And finally, by the last reconstruction, which followed after the earthquake in 1979, the cathedral got its original appearance. There are valuable and rare items of movables and art kept in the cathedral. The item of great importance is a high ciborium from the second half of the 14th century, a work created in the workshop of Fra Vito of Kotor. The lateral apses hold Gothic sculptures, and the four marble altars from the 18th century were produced in Venice. There is also a masterpiece of Kotor`s goldsmith`s trade - a gold-plated silver plate. In the church treasury valuable examples of easel paintings, religious works by domestic (Lovro Dobričević) and foreign (Bassano the Elder, Michael Neidlinger) authors are kept. In the church reliquary numerous relics such as the silver casket and the "holy head" of St. Tryphon are also kept. There are also votive objects of diverse shapes by Kotor' s goldsmiths created between the 15th and 20th century.

It is situated on Piazza Greca in Kotor and it best testifies the harmonious life of both Catholic and Orthodox people over the centuries. It is a Romanesque structure, moderate and proportional. It was erected and painted at the end of the 12th century. By the end of the 17th century, it belonged to the Catholics when, due to wars and the arrival of great number of people in Kotor, it was given up to the Orthodox people to use it. By the end of 19th century there were two altars, Catholic and Orthodox. From that time there is an iconostasis by famous local authors and well-known Kotor' s goldsmiths who decorated some parts of it.

St. Nicholas Church - Kotor

St. Tryphon`s Cathedral

St. Tryphon`s Cathedral

The bell tower on the photo is of the Chapel Our Lady of Rosary. Andrija Zmajević erected it as his own mausoleum in 1678. The style characteristics of the Renaissance and Baroque can be recognised on the church as well as on the bell tower and palace. Near the church there is the thin octagonal bell tower, among the most beautiful ones on the Adriatic coast, and it is supposed to have been made according to the project of Andrija Zmajević.

Budva - Old Town

The town of Budva is situated on a small peninsula, the former island that is connected to the land by means of sandbanks. The first Illyrian settlement was mentioned in the 4th century under Greek name of Budhoe. Budva dates from the 5th century BC. The town shared the destiny of other coastal towns dominated by the Illyrians, Byzantine, Romans, Serbian countries, Turkey, Venetian Republic and Austria. Each of them left its civilization trace on this territory.

According to legend, Budva was established by son of the Phoenician King Kadmo, who was banished from Teba.

The legend says that in today's Budva, on the Adriatic coast he came by bullock`s team.

Enheleans headed by Kadmo won battle against Illyrians and Kadmo became Illyrian ruler. Later on, he led Illyrians and

Enheleans into war against Greece where he conquered many cities, until his army sinned against Delta`s sanctuary.

Kadmo and Harmonija, by God's decision, had been transformed into snakes.

Budva is the only Montenegrin town mentioned in a classical, antique legend. The great philosopher Sophocles had called Budva ``the town of the Illyrians``. Budva is a centre of the Montenegrin tourism. Its beautiful beaches made according to all world standards, numerous classy restaurants, outdoor terraces and discotheques will satisfy the needs of even those most demanding clients and in particular the needs of the young population. Budva is famous for its rich cultural-artistic programme that has been living for two decades in the form of "Budva-Theatre City", "Poets` Square" etc.

Budva`s image is enriched by St.Nikola island, where church having the same name is

Budva - satelit

Bečići - satelit

situated, built before the XVI century, restructured in 1864.

In the Old Town located St.Ivan church from the VII century, where protector of the city, so called **Budva`s Madonna** is kept, dating from the end of the XIV century.

Nine monasteries are located at the Budva`s Riviera:

Podlastva - located towards Kotor, 3,5 km away from Budva. It was built by Czar Dusan in 1350. In 1417 it was mentioned for the first time. Monastery complex consists of the church dedicated to Madonna`s birth and shelters.

Podostrog -located 2 km north from the Old city under the hill called Ostrog. The Monastery was built in the XV century. Bishop Danilo Petrovic was its regular visitor, Petar II Petrovic Njegos, who in sacred silence of this place, wrote his book "Svobodijada" and some parts of "Gorski vijenac". The Monastery terrace with the sea view, island St. Nikola built by metropolitan Sava Petrovic, reconstructed by Petar II Petrovic Njegos, make this place more beautiful.

Podmaine - has monastery church dedicated to St. Petka.

Monastery Stanjevici - situated above the village Pobori, for the first time mentioned in 1714. The first Montenegrin Code of Petar I was for the first time adopted in this monastery in 1798. It was destroyed by the Austrians in 1868.

Monastery Vojnići - consists of two churches dedicated to St. Dimitrije and St. Nikola. It was built in the XV century.

Monastery Duljevo - built in the XIV century, in the period of Czar Dusan`s reign, and it was closely connected with the monastery called Visoki Decani.

Monastery Reževići - consists of two churches, shelter and ruins of the third one. The first church, built by Stefan Prvovjencani in the XII century, is dedicated to The Ascnesion

In 1935, in Paris, the beach of Becici was proclamed to be the most beautiful beach in Europe.

of Madonna. Besides another church, built at start of the XIX century, there is a specific bell tower. In the third church there are remains of mural painting. It was established by Czar Dusan in the XIV century, and it is dedicated to St. Stefan.

Monastery Gradište

consists of a shelter and 3 churches. It was built on the remains of some antic construction. The main church is dedicated to St. Nikola, and other two are dedicated successively to St. Sava and The Ascnesion of Madonna. It was established in the XII century.

Monastery Praskvica - is situated near from St. Stefan, above Milocer beach. It was established by Vojislav, King of Zeta, in 1050. The most reliable historical source about monastery`s foundation dates from 1413. French destroyed the whole monastery in 1812. Thanks to big donation from Pastrovici and Russians help, church was renovated in 1847. It consists of two churches, an old and new shelter and "small tower" which once was a school.

In the Gallery of the Archeological Museum of Budva (St. Maria` s church houses it) there are numerous remains of the material and spiritual culture of this beautiful town and area.

Sea depth in the Budva bay along the coast varies from 35 m, and later it transformes into sandy bottom. Sea temperature in summer time amounts about 25ºC, while in winter months is 13 ºC and over. Sea visibility is from 15-35 m, which makes this location a real challenge for divers. Budva Riviera covers the area of 38 km jagged coast with many lagoons, sandy beaches and bays.

The most famous beaches of Budva Riviera are Jaz 1200 m, Slovenska plaza 1600 m, Mogren I i II 350 m, Becici 1950 m, Przno 260m, Milocer 280 m, Kamenovo 330 m, Sveti Stefan 700 m, Drobni pijesak 240 m, Petrovac 600 m,

Budva - Old Town

Budva - Concerts

Theater city - detail

Grad teatar - detalj   *Mogren I i II*

Lucice 220 m, Buljarice 1980 m.

The biggest settlements in Budva Riviera are: Budva with 10 000 residents, Petrovac with 4 000, St. Stefan with almost 2 000 and Becici with about 1 500 residents.

Budva Riviera has many plants of olives, mandarins, lemon, orange, pomegranate, and flora that dominates - palms, cactus, agaves, mimosa.

The aquatorium of Budva is rich with flora and fauna. Sea fish that can be found here are: tooth fish, sea-bass, red fish, sea-bream, gold fish.

Budva has over 2300 sunny hours, sea-bath season lasts for 182 days, from 10 May to the middle of November.

Depending on season in Budva blows: - bura, north wind blowing from the continental area and bringing sunny weather; jugo, southern wind blowing from the sea to the continental part and bringing rain; maestral, north-west summer wind bringing refreshness in summer time; pulenat, Lebiš, Tramuntana, Levanat

Budva

The Orthodox Church of Holy Trinity from 1804, Budva (the bell tower of the Catholic Cathedral from the 15th century in the back).

Sveti Stefan - Panorama

Budva

Budva

Petrovac

Perast

Petrovac the city on the Montenegrin seaside, located south-east from Budva. This settlement was developed along with the Venecian Kastel Lastve, and until 1919 the whole settlement was named like that.

Name Lastva was for the first time mentioned in "Chronicle of Doclea`s Pope". Fortress Kastio, building Lazaret are built in period of reign of Venetians in the XV and in the XVI century. The settlement started to get its present form at the end of the XVIII century and at the begining of the XIX century. Near Petrovac, there are two little islands Katic and Sveta Nedjelja /Sacred Sunday/.

The legend says that the church St.Nedjelja was built by sailors` donations and other legend says that was built by greek sailor, who`s ship had crashed, and he found his salvation on that place, on saint day Sunday.

41

Sveti Stefan

"...Just as if I have returned to the town from the most beautiful fairy tale of my childhood." - said the Italian movie star Sophia Lauren visiting St. Stefan.

Sutomore - beach

Bar city and port at the Montenegro seaside. Bar was for the first time mentioned in the IX century. In the early Middle Age is a part of the Bizantium Empire. In 1183, it was conquered by Stefan Nemanja. The reign of Nemanjic family was flourishing time for the city. In 1443 it became part of Venice, in 1571 it was conquered by Turks. Montenegrians liberated it in 1878.

The port of Bar is one of the biggest ports in this part of Europe and it has huge economic importance for Montenegro and the region.

At the foot of the mountain Rumija, 3-4 km away from the sea the ancient town of Bar is placed. Its turbulent history remained many significant monuments- ramparts of the old town of Bar, remains of the Benedictine monastery on the Cape of Ratac from 11th century, St. Tekla`s Church in Sutomore, from 12th century (the church has two altars- an Orthodox and a Catholic).

King Nicola wrote the following lines to glorify the moment of "**wedding of Montenegro and the sea**"

"I greet you, sea the great,
Oh, valley, fluent and flat,
You, chamber the giant,
Our desire of ancient times"

At the beginning of the 20th century, at the same time it got the port, Bar also got the first railway (running from Pristan to Skadar Lake), and it entered the Guinness book of records thanks to the village called Limljani that will be remembered by the greatest number of railway stations in the world. Beside the port and narrow gage railroad Bar also got the first radio-telegraphic station in the Balkans at that time.

Bar

The widest and oldest planted gardens of olive trees are placed in Bar. Some of the trees are up to 2000 years old. The fact that olive trees must be planted by human hand naturally led to conclusion that there must have been many **hard-working people** to plant and cultivate them, of which more than 50% are older than the time Bar was found, and that survived up to the present days together with the secret of Vladimir´s cross (the legend of Vladimir and Kosara).

One of the oldest olive trees in the world- the Old Olive, is located at the foot of the mountain Lisinje, in Mirovica under the walls of the old town of Bar where different civilizations found their shelter or home to live in.

One of the oldest olive trees in the world - the Old Olive in Bar, older than 2000 years.

The importance of this tree is that it represents a priceless and irreplaceable part of both visual and spiritual identity of the town. It is over two millennia old, with the scope of 10m and with, even today, fruity treetop. There are numberless stories and legends related to this tree and its effects, and one of the most beautiful, after this place was named, says that feuds between families used to be settled underneath this olive tree.

Under its old treetop, the International children festival called **"Gatherings under the Old Olive"** has been held for almost 20 years, together with **"Chronicle of Bar"**, the Summer festival that became a trademark of the town under Rumija and not only in the culture of Montenegro.

The biggest olive yards can be found in Montenegro, with olive trees 2000 years old.

Utjeha

MONTENEGRO COAST

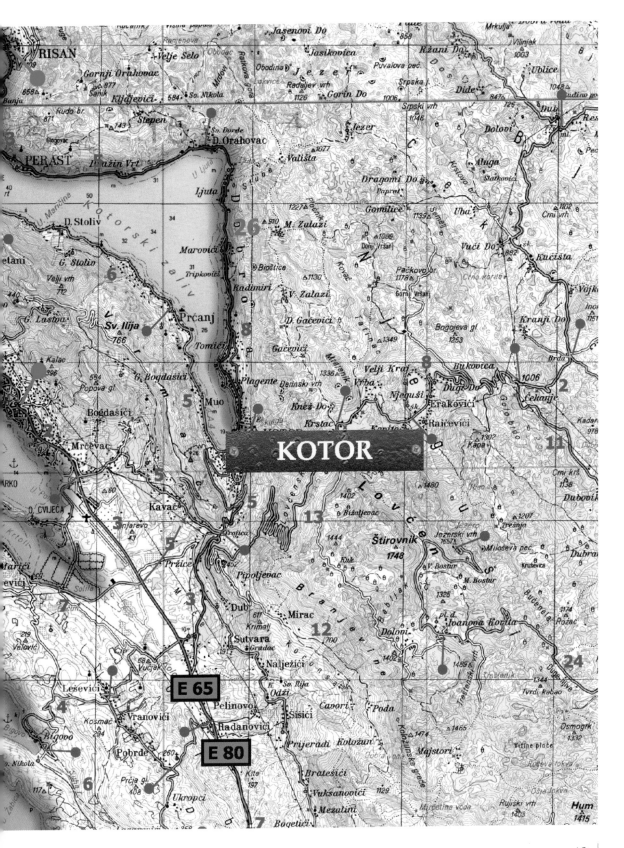

KOTOR

E 851

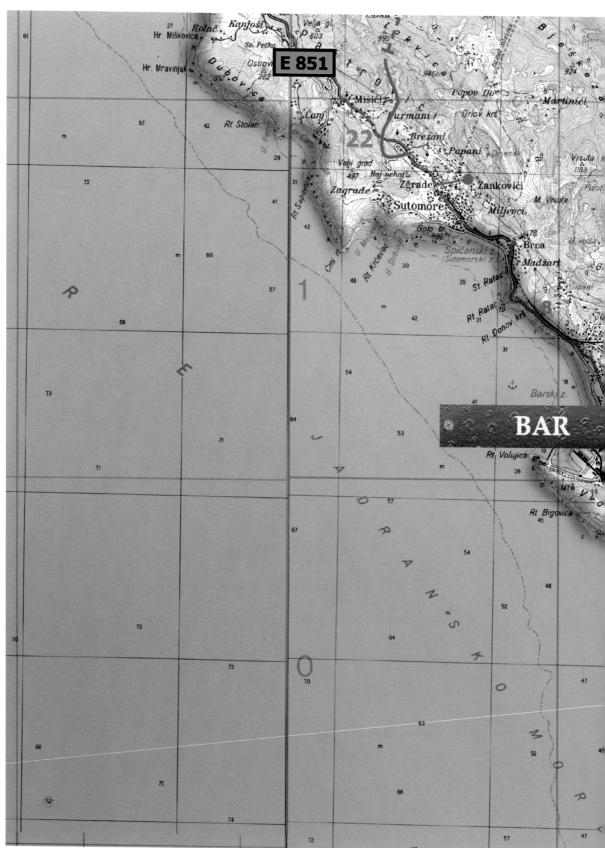

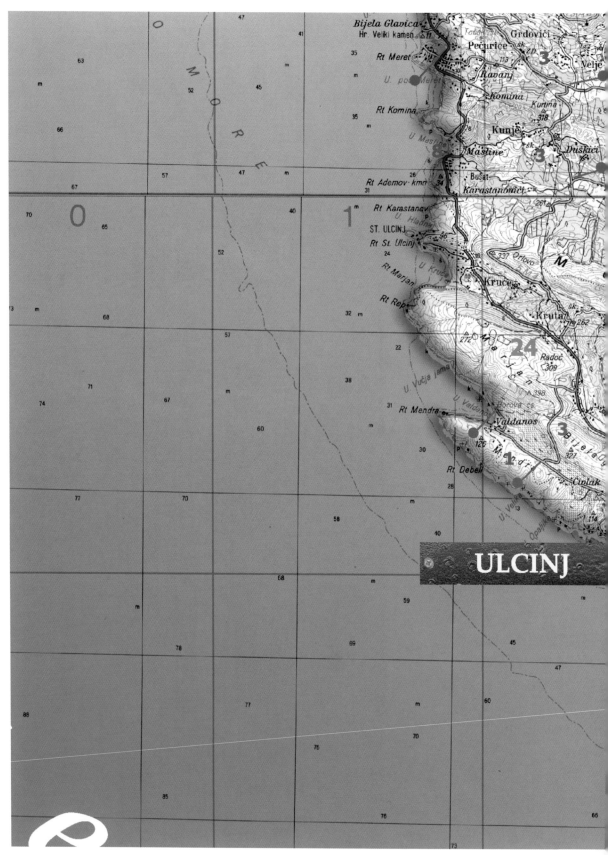

ULCINJ

Ulcinj is located in the southest part of the Adriatic Sea. The oldest part of the city sank during a strong earthquake that occurred in 1444. Today`s Old City, dating from XII century, is surrounded by walls. The New City oriental architecture was saved.

Big salt works are situated in the Port of Milena. Ulcinj was for a long time a pirates' nest and their commander Utudž Alija was a nightmare for trade ships in the Mediterranean and Adriatic Sea. In 1675, Turkish navy with its leader Sulejman-paša sank the entire Ulcinj`s pirates navy. Enormous robbed fortune vanished in the sea.

There is a legend according to which Servantes, who served as a convict in casemates of Ulcinj, had a dream of an unknown Dulcineja girl - a girl from Ulcinj.

The longest beach in the Adriatic Sea is a 12500 m-long beach called Velika plaža, near Ulcinj. It spreads from Patislava peninsula to river Bojana`s delta.

Under the name of Colhainium, Ulcinj first mentioned Plimije the Older. Although it was liberated from the Turkish control in 1878 at the same time as Bar, it became part of Montenegro only after the decisions made on Berlin Congress in 1878 under great military pressure and constant diplomatic activity of allies. After the Navy had blocked Ulcinj and the greatest Turkish port Izmir, Smirna in Small Asia, only then Porta signed the joining of Ulcinj to Montenegro.

The settlement of Šas or **Svač on Lake of Šas** (first mentioned in 1067 as a bishop town) was built on **the Roman road Olcinium**- Skodra yet in the Illyrian time. The symbol of town- a three-floo red for-

Ulcinj

tress built in the Renaissance style was found on the money coined in this town in the 14th century.

According to the legends (Justinijan 1533) there were as many churches in the town as there are days of the year. Today, it is a popular picnic area of Ulcinj.

*The longest beach in the Adriatic Sea is a 12500 m-long beach called **Velika plaža**, near Ulcinj. It spreads from Patislava peninsula to river Bojana`s delta.*

The biggest salt works factory of the former Yugoslavia has been built in Ulcinj and has the record production of 44.000 tones of salt.

Ulcinj is the sunniest city in the Montenegro seaside, with the average of 2550 sunny hours per annum.

 Skadarsko lake

THE HINTERLANDS OF COAST

Cetinje. You can hardly find another place in the world where altitude difference (from 0 to 1500m) has been so skillful performed, **on a shorter distance**, as it is case with the old road Cetinje- Njegusi-Cetinje famous for its serpentines. In the old 1884, the beauty and nobility of the Queen Milena enchanted the architect of this unusual, winding road so that he used two serpentines to create letter M, the beginning letter of her name, to pay respect to her. This rare road leads to the native house of one of the greatest

Lovćen mausoleum

"There the words lack. There, too, I have to become speechless and enjoy."
Bernard Shaw visiting Lovćen

Lovćen

Slavic poets, Petar II Petrović Njegoš and further to Cetinje, the old capital and the town of museums.

Cetinje is located under Lovcen mountain, on 680 m above sea-level. Ivan Crnojevic built its palace under Orlov krš in 1482, two years later he built Cetinje monastery. In that way he made basis of fure Montenegrin state.

Cetinje had never been conquered by Turks, even they had been attacking it for 3 times.

In 1692, when Turks pushed trough Cetinje monastery's door, Montenegrins enlighted

Asked why he didn`t want to be buried on the highest peak of Lovćen, Štirovnik at 1749 m altitude but on a smaller Jezerski peak at 1675 m altitude, he answered:
"A greater Montenegrin than me will be born one day."

In 1935, it has been raining continuously for 27 days in Cetinje.

the gun powder hidden in monastery and together with the attackers and monastery blew themselves up.

Palace Biljarda built in 1839 is in the city's forum, and its name was given after the billiard - Njegos's favourite game.

There are also Knezev palace, Zetski dom, Vladin dom. The most beautiful building in Cetinje, built in 1910, is building of French embassy. The story says, that at the same time building of French embassy in Cairo was pro-

Cetinje

Peter II Petrović (1813-1851),
a bishop and a ruler of Montenegro, was
born in Njeguši, a pleasant village at the foot
of Lovćen. As a ruler he managed to set the
circumstances in the country, he established
the court, introduced a tax, established the
Senate, abolished the "guvernadurstvo"
(noble title) and he founded the first Elementary School and Printing Shop in 1834. As a
poet he achieved the greatness only few can.
His most famous works are: "The Mountain
Wreath", "Light of the Microcosm", "The mir-
ror of the Serbs" and "False Tsar Šćepan the
Little" and "Svobodijada". He was buried on
one of the peaks of Lovćen.

Njegoš' s native house

Flag from Vucji dol

At the entrance of the Mausoleum, there is Njegos`s statue chiseled in black granite with an eagle, a symbol of freedom and height above it, and with a book, that celebrated him, on his lap.

"Octoich" printed in the "Obod Printing Shop" in 1494 also known as "Crnojević Printing Shop", the first South-Slav state printing shop in the world. The printing and decorating of the "Octoich" was done by seven monks and supervised by monk Makarije.

Njegos's original last resting place was a small chapel (from 1845) that had been damaged, demolished and instead of it in 1974, Mausoleum was erected to pay respect to this great poet. 461 stairs and 80 m long tunnel are leading to the Mausoleum.

jected and that plan with oriental notes was replaced by mistake and instead of Egypt arrived in Montenegro, and Montenegrin stone building went to Egypt forever. According to the available information, Cetinje was first mentioned in 1440. Before the Turkish invasions, in 1475, the capital of Zeta had been moved from Žabljak (on Skadar Lake) to Obod near Crnojevića River, and finally to Cetinje.

Many educational and enlightening decisions were made on Montenegrin court. Due to its special importance, it`s worth mentioning the decision made on the formation of **"The First State Printing House in the world"** in 1493, founded by Đurđe Crnojević, the last ruler of Zeta who possessed particular sense of culture judging by his testament written in Italian. In the place called Obod in 1494, a monk Makarije printed the first book called "The Octoich of the First Voice", only 33 years later than the first book was printed (the Bible printed in Gutenberg`s printing shop in Majnc in 1455).

Asked why he didn`t want to be buried on the highest peak of Lovćen, Štirovnik at 1749 m altitude but on a smaller Jezerski peak at 1675 m altitude, he answered: "A greater Montenegrin than me will be born one day."

The history of hotel industry started in Cetinje, Montenegro in 1864 when the first hotel called "Lokanda" was built (today, it is "Grand Hotel"). It was not only the hospitality center but also the center of culture and entertaining life of the old capital. The First Elementary School of Montenegro, compulsory for all children, was founded in Cetinje in 1833, then the first National Association of Red Cross (1876) was also formed here and then the first car imported and used for delivering post on the international relation Cetinje- Kotor (Montenegro - Austro-Hungary).

On Lovćen (the National Park of 2000 hectares) on Jezerski Peak, the mausoleum of Petar II Petrović Njegoš, a ruler, a poet and a bishop was erected according to the design of the sculptor Ivan Meštrović, at an altitude of 1657 m that makes it one of the monuments of the highest altitude in Europe.

Smoked ham, smoked sheep meat and mead of Njeguši are just some of the numerous local specialties that are together with hospitality of the local people offered to a tourist in the architecturally authentic objects of this area.

Podgorica - Milenijum bridge

Podgorica. There are only few capital cities in the world with this characteristic: you can get to the seaside for 40 minutes , and also, going to opposite direction you can get on 2000 m above sea-level for 40 minutes. This city is at the same time the capital city of Montenegro and its name is Podgorica.

Podgorica was for the first time mentioned on 18 August in 1326. Podgorica is situated on 44 m above sea-level in Zeta valley. It is one of the warmest cities in Europe, with 42

In 1493, only 4 decades after Gutemberg, printing office started its travel from Venice to Cetinje by command of Zeta's monarch Djuradj Crnojevic. Printing office has existed for 3 years, from 1493-1496.
Oktoih prvoglasnik /Octoechos, first voice/, Oktoih Petoglasnik /Octo-echos, fifth voice/, Psaltir, Trebnik and tetraevangelion were printed from 1493 to 1496.

°C temperature in the summer time. Administrative and transit center of Montenegro has five rivers to refresh its residents in hot summers: Zeta, Moraca, Ribnica, Sitnica and Cijevna.

The capital of Montenegro is Podgorica founded at the location of the ancient Doclea and medieval river Ribnica.

After the World War II, this town was erected out of the ruins *(**Podgorica was bombed 76 times in the period 1941-1945, of which no one can be proud**).*

Today, it is a modern city with avenues,

Podgorica has changed its name five times. In the Roman Time it was known as Birzinium, in the Podgorica, since 1946 as Titograd and finally in the 21st century (that is since 1992) it got its pres

s Ribnica, in the 14th century as
jorica.

Monument to Pushkin, the city of Moscow gifted the city of Podgorica

Podgorica has 2.460 sunny days a year (while Venice has 2.350). A month with the least sunny hours is December with 108 while July has most sunny hours 334. The most common winds in Podgorica are the northern that blows 22,2% and the southern of 13,1%. Due to its location in the valley, out of all measurements made in Podgorica 45% goes for silence unlike Bar where 23% goes for it.

Average minimal and maximal temperatures for Podgorica:

	spring	summer	autmn	winter
Min	9,4	19,3	11,8	2,4
Max	19,6	31,0	21,5	10,3

Duklja
1ST century BC

Cijevna River emerges in the territory of Albania. The total length of its flow is 39 km of which 32 km is in the territory of Montenegro. (It was named after its riverbed that looks like the pipe - in Montenegrin "cijev"="pipe").

Marko Miljanov (1833-1901) (Duke from Kuci and writer). The legend says that Marko killed wolf with his own hands when he was still 14 years old boy, and when he was 51 he learnt to write and read.

"All fine features of Montenegrins can be found in the character of Marko Miljanov, but none of their shortcomings."
Joseph Holechek

Museum of Marko Miljanov Medun, Kuci

bridges and parks and traffic, educational, political, economic, trade and culture centre of Montenegro. Podgorica is among the cities of better traffic connection in the territory of former Yugoslavia thanks to its airports, railways and radial lined roads. Vacation and recreation areas of the Mareza, the Morača canyon, the Cijevna, the Plavnica on the lake and many others provide the recreation of the highest level.

Podgorica is situated at the crossroads of several important traffic roads that "meet" in the valleys of the Zeta, Morača and Cijevna, in the ravine of Skadar Lake and in the vicinity of the Adriatic Sea, in the pleasant climate conditions of the plain.

Podgorica, former Ribnica, had a strong economy. Firm and developed commercial links between Dubrovnik and state of Nemanjići

went via Trebinje and Nikšić to Podgorica. Situated at the most frequent crossroads, Podgorica was the centre of constant circulation of goods, traders, couriers and other travellers, which improved its development, economic and military power and strategic importance. Economic, cultural and artistic rise of the town was interrupted by Turkish occupation in 1474. The Turks erected a large fortress and out of a former settlement with developed commercial connections made their central defense and attack bastion towards disobedient tribes. They managed to withstand all the attacks thanks to the fortified town with towers, gates and defensive ramparts.

According to the decision made on Berlin Congress in 1878, Podgorica was adjoined Montenegro. At the same time it meant the

Đurđevi stupovi

end of the Ottoman occupation and the beginning of a new period in the development of both Podgorica and Montenegro. In a relatively short time, the city made a big progress and became a strong market. The first forms of the concentration of capital emerged. In 1904, the first financial institute, Zeta' s Savings Bank was founded that soon after developed into Bank of Podgorica. The new roads to all surrounding towns were built and in 1902, Podgorica got the first more significant enterprise, the Factory of tobacco.

In the period between two world wars, Podgorica had 13,000 inhabitants.

Under the name of Titograd, on 13th July, it was declared the capital of the Republic, which also meant the beginning of new life. The following period brought complete transformation to the town. Material, personnel and scientific-technical potential was enlarged, great educational development, different culture and health institutes founded while the town became connected to all parts of the country and abroad thanks to modern traffic roads and airlines. In that way Titograd became commercial, social-economic and culture centre of Montenegro.

On 2nd April 1992, the town again got its former name of Podgorica.

Archeological sites in the territory of Podgorica:

Medun dates from 3rd century BC. Old town of Medun (Meteon), more a fortress than a town, situated 13 km away from Podgorica in its northern -east part, dates from the ancient times

It was first erected as a fortress and then later between 4th and 3rd centuries BC as a town. Well-preserved walls made of large blocks of

Roman legions occupied Medun around 167, and on that occasion the last Illyrian king Gentije and his family were captured.

chiseled stone were set in several lines. By its firmness and proportion, this construction greatly differs from other less important Illyrian towns.

From culture-artistic point of view, very interesting are two excavations in the rock on the way from the down to the upper town. It is supposed that that was a place where rites related to snake cult used to take place. According to the Illyrian's belief snake was a symbol of a myth ancestor. In the north of the upper town there is a necropolis. It dates from the Illyrian age, but it hasn` t been examined.

Roman legions occupied Medun around 167, and on that occasion the last Illyrian king Gentije and his family were captured.

Medun hasn` t been studied enough yet.

Beside its interesting, rich and distant past, it is also interesting as an object for examining all culture stages from prehistory to Middle Age. At the foot of the walls of this town and fortress, our famous writer, a tribe leader, a Montenegrin duke and a hero Marko Miljanov lived. He was buried in the acropolis in front of the small church.

Docleati, a folk of Illyrian origin dating from the 1st century BC, founded the town of Doclea.

It was situated in the northern -west, 3 km away from Podgorica, on the flat plateau between the rivers Zeta and Morača. At that time, it was a big town with 8,000-10,000 inhabitants and with solved elementary public services such as: water supply, sewerage system and streets. Roman control was strengthened in the territory of Doclea when their legions occupied the town in the 1st century, after their long and exhausting struggles with the Illyrians. During the Roman dominance, the town

Skadarsko jezero

SKO JEZERO
(LJIĆENI I ŠKODRES)

sko jezero

rapidly and suddenly progressed so that it soon became political, cultural and religious centre of the province of Prevalis with municipal laws, which all greatly influenced the change of the population structure and social-economic relations. The arrival of the new people meant the "opening" of the town especially towards the Adriatic coast. The commercial relations with Italy, Dalmatia and East regions started to strengthen and later also with Macedonia and Greece.

At the beginning of the 6th century, there was a catastrophic earthquake in Doclea, and in 609, it was robbed and again demolished by the Avars and the Slavs. The name of Doclea was mentioned for a long time later but since the 10th century, it was more known under the name of Zeta.

Podgorica has a surface of about 1,500 square kilometers that is 10,7 % of the territory of the Republic of Montenegro.

The Adriatic greatly influences the climate of Podgorica. That influence comes along the river Bojana and over Skadar Lake. Due to the surrounding mountains the Mediterranean climate has changed and Podgorica has altered Mediterranean climate characterized by warm and hot summers and rainy winters. Thanks to the thermal influences of the Adriatic, Podgorica has high air temperatures in winter.

Average annual air temperature in Podgorica is 16,4°C, maximal is 40,7°C and minimal -4,6°C.

Average annual precipitation in Podgorica is 1544 mm/ m², and relative air humidity is 59,6%.

On average there are 118 rainy, 3 snowy and with strong wind 58 days a year.

Along the Zeta River near Podgorica, there is Bjelopavlićka plain. This is the area where the old town of Spuž is located which used to be

Žabljak Crnojevića

Monastery Ostrog

a constant cause of fights between the Turks and the Montenegrins who both wanted dominance over it. Unfortunately, due to its closeness to Podgorica, this town is mostly abandoned and its population scattered to

Podgorica and other towns so that it houses the Institute of Sentence Execution (ISE) today.

Danilovgrad lies in the pleasant valley of the river Zeta. It was founded in 1869 by the idea of King Nikola, and it got its name after Prince Danilo Petrovic.

Manastir Ostrog, was erected in 1650. Donji i Gornji Monasteries form it.

The Ostrog Cave had been entrusted with safeguarding Gornji Ostrog, lying on 900 m altitude sea-level, while the hands of believers built the "spiritual nest" of the Montenegrin nation. The Monastery was a Holy Theophany of Stojan Jovanović – St. Vasilije Ostroski, man from Hercegovina, Metropolitan of Zahum-Hercegovina area. Today, relics of St. Vasilije Ostroški, considered to have healing power, are kept in Gornji Ostrog. The relics of St. Vasilije Ostroški were severel times moved from the monastery: 1853, 1877, 1914, 1941 and 1999.

The Ostrog Monastery is the most visited sanctuary at this territory. It is visited by all believers regardless of religion.

Morača Monastery

NATIONAL PARKS
AND CANYON

There are four national parks in Montenegro-Skadar Lake, Lovćen, Biogradsko Lake and Durmitor. Durmitor with the Tara canyon and town of Kotor are under the protection of UNESCO.

Skadar Lake is the largest lake on the Balkans with 40 islands in it. Depending on water level and season, the space of Skadar Lake varies from 391 to 540 square kilometers. `Skadar mud`, as the local people call it, has as many `eyes` (fountains) as there are islands in it. The deepest of them is Raduš at the depth of about 65m.

Well-known ornithology stations in Europe are located on Skadar Lake and on nearby Šasko Lake of 3,4 square kilometers. There are 666 birds` kinds that inhabit different parts of Europe and 508 kinds of that number inhabit these two lakes or their direct vicinity. The richness in birds` kinds of this area is best seen when it is compared to Great Britain where there are 422 birds` kinds. A rarity of all Europe called *"nesit pelecanus onocratolus"* inhabits Skadar Lake. It is around 180 cm long and even up to 2,6 m long with spread wings.

Rich areas for game animals hunting, enclosed hunting fields and fishing areas attract hunters, tourists, fishers and ornithologists from all over the world. *The lake is supplied with clean water from its tributaries the Morača River and Crnojevića River, and along the wide course of the navigable river of Bojana it empties into the sea.* At the mouth of Ada Bojana, there are pleasant raft-restaurants placed famous for fish specialties and particularly attractive to tourists- gastronomes from all over the world.

The coastal area of Skadar Lake (a pleasant, picturesque area of Crmnica and a sandy, sunny Ćemovsko field) has developed a traditional and widely recognized production of **Vranac** vine- at present, recognizable and irreplaceable Montenegrin brand on the international market. Crypto-depression is a natural feature of Skadar Lake as at some places its bottom is 30 m under the level of the Adriatic Sea.

Little less than **2/3 of Skadar Lake** belongs to the territorial waters of Montenegro and the rest to Albania. The north of Montenegro is a mountain area intersected by the canyons and gorges of the rivers and by fertile picturesque valleys placed between them.

The north of Montenegro is a mountainous area intersected by the canyons and gorges of the rivers and by fertile picturesque valleys placed between them.

The Morača Canyon

Its most interested part is called Platije (35 km long), the limestone -dolomite furrow where the Morača River broke its bed through 800-1000m high and steep cliffs. The adventurous tourists who travel through this canyon will encounter often changing of tunnels, passages and bridges accompanied by changing of different feelings of admiring, fear and curiosity. You will get the impression as if you have just entered the stage of stoned game and, at the same time, the `talkative` history of this unusual people where the capricious Morača has the leading role. As an accidental witness of the turbulent history, Morača Monastery emerged at one of the plateaus, at the place where the canyon is gently curved. It is the oldest religious object (erected in 1252) in this territory and the remainder of medieval building school of Raška. The first cycle of frescoes of this mono-nave church was created in the 12th century and the second cycle in the 17th century as the church was without roof more than 70 years during the 16th century after the Turks had used it to make bullets for fights. The frescoes from the 12th century, inspired by the prophet Elijah, are the most important. It is also the only saved example of the medieval paintings that describes the prophet Elijah.

The Morača River is 97,1 km long, and with its tributary the Zeta River has the largest surface of river basin in Montenegro (3200 square kilometers). These two rivers also form the biggest water flow (1510 Q m³/sec).

The National Park **Biogradska gora** (one of two jungles in Europe) was founded in 1652 in the vicinity of the mountain town Kolašin. It includes 4.000 hectares of the surface of the Bjelasica, of which 2600 hectares are covered with forests and inhabited by deer, roe deer, boars, bears wild cats and mouflons, while the rest are pastures and meadows. There are 25 habitats of plants and 84 kinds of trees. Giant trees are up to 60 m tall. In the central part of

Kasoronj (Trupa Longicuria) is a plant which can be only found in Scadar Lake. Even its roots always resides in water, it can not give fruits without rains in the summer time.

that luxury nature, at an altitude of 1094m Biogradsko Lake is situated, whose water space depending on water level is up to 250.000 square kilometers. Kapetansko Lake and Manito Lake are situated above it at an altitude of 1687m. Pleasant surroundings of the lake and forests of the national park are outstanding tourist motives - air spa, ski runs, swimming and rowing in the lake. This great tourist potential hasn`t been completely valorized yet. The authentic national restaurants provide local specialties such as homemade `kajmak`(dairy cream), `cicvara`, `kačamak`, smoked ham, lamb and venison cooked under a bell.

On the way Podgorica - Bijelo Polje through the canyon of the Morača River and through the valleys of the Tara River to Mojkovac and of the Lim River and downstream from B. Polje, a part of Beograd-Bar railway is placed reaching near Kolašin an altitude of almost 1029m. Passing through 104 tunnels (43 km) and over 90 bridges, this railroad is a true constructing wonder, and the bridge on Mala rijeka, the tributary of the Morača River, is the highest railroad bridge in Europe thanks to its height of 200m.

The town of Mojkovac is located in the green amphitheatric valley, on the very winding shore of the river Tara and reminds on a fisherman who is patiently standing above the water. It was named after the money coined there - `My coined money`. Mojkovac is one of the oldest mining settlements. The people of Sax used to dig lead and zinc for the Serbian rulers` account in the early Middle age.

The length of the shore of the Biogradsko Lake is 3,300m and it takes an hour walk to go around it by the pedestrian path. The lake is 875m large and the biggest depth is 12,10m.

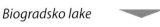

Biogradsko lake

During the First World War, this was the place where the Montenegrins covered Serbian retreat over Montenegro and Albania to Corfu. Losing from more numerous and powerful enemy and reducing the number of their soldiers, the Montenegrins managed to cover Serbian retreat for 45 days. Today, the hill above Mojkovac where that historical battle took place is famous for record quantities of strawberries and blackberries that children sell to travellers earning in that way their pocket money during the summer.

The valley of the Tara River leads to another famous mountain center, Žabljak on Durmitor.

Durmitor is the first national park.

It was recognized as that in 1952. Park is 39.000 hectares large and includes four municipalities - Žabljak, Pljevlja, Šavnik and

Mojkovac (4120 residents) was established by King Uros in 1250. In the period of King Uros`s reign, Mojkovac was bigger city than London in that time.

Mojkovac. The deepest cave of 898m is located on Durmitor. This national park is larger than all national parks of Croatia, or than all of Bosnia and Slovenia together. It includes the ecological reservation of the Tara basin, the only one in the territory of former Yugoslavia, that is according to criterion of `a man and a biosphere` accepted by UNESCO among 57 world`s national parks, and registered on 1st February 1977 due to exceptional importance of `this natural zone` and its genetic reserves.

The Tara Canyon is, due to its 1300m high sides, the deepest in Europe and second in the world, after the Colorado Canyon in the USA. The Tara is the largest river (141 km) of Montenegro (belongs to Black Sea basin), together with the Piva River and the Morača River form `the grand canyon zone of Europe`, and thanks to many traffic arteries made on

Kolašin

Peak of Prutaš - Durmitor

On average there are 138 snowy days a year in Žabljak, and the highest depth of the snow measured in the very town was 210 cm.

Žabljak - 1450 m; Durmitor in the back - 2522 m

Tara - detail

Black Lake

Hridsko lake

Black Lake is the largest lake on Durmitor mountain and it is situated at an altitude of 1442 m. It is 1155 m long and 810 m wide. Large Lake and Small Lake form Black Lake and when the water level falls off during the summer they set apart. Large Lake is 24,5 m and Small Lake is 49,1 m deep.

Black Lake

Pešić' s Lake *- Its altitude is 1820m, the surface 37,400m², and the depth 8,4m. It is the second lake by surface on Bjelasica Mountain.*

Large Ursulovačko Lake *is situated in the central part of Bjelasica at an altitude of 1895m. Its surface is 12,200m² and it is 8,1m deep.*

their passages and valleys they are available to those who want to come to watch and enjoy. The Tara River has its headwaters in a village at 1850m above sea level. It is also called `the tear of Europe` as it has been proclaimed the cleanest river of Europe by experts` analysis.

According to the famous naturalist Jovan Cvijić, the Komovi represents one of the greatest hydrological centres in the Balkans. The spring of the Tara seems as if it, almost deliberately, hides its tracks in the mountain crags where from running upstream along the constant and more powerful springs of the Mokra River it speeds up along the Veruša River (15 km) and reaches the summer pasture of Maglič (at an altitude of 1860m) or not less famous river of this area, the Opasanica (12 km), placed under the very peak of Kom and made of more springs, of which Bijela voda is the most famous and where one cannot drain over two-three sips of `white` water, and finally under the Planinac (2153 m).

Like two sisters who visit their native house, the Veruša and the Opasanica "meet" at Han Garančic where they form the Tara River.

It is much harder to single out Kom from the Kom` s area than Durmitor from Sinjajevina as it is not a "foreign body" on that valley but the highest crest of that mountain range. By its scope Sinjajevina exceeds Durmitor if we observe it as a separated massif, and its sprouts, roots or `feet` as people call them end in the depth of Bjelasica, in the north from Kolašin, Zeletina and the Visitor near the town of Plav. The mountain ranges opposite the Lim River in capricious and sudden changes separate the sky with the Albanian Alps (the Prokletije).

Kom represents the key point where from valleys and sprouts are reflecting like the first morning sunshine. In the north, those are plateaus between the towns of Kolašin and Andrijevica with the range of the mountains Ključ, Bač and Bjelasica, in the east, the mountains between the rivers Perućica and Lim and in the west, the narrow steep chain between Maglić and Black mountain that represents a link to the mountain of Žijevo.

Kom is a steep, rocky and light green crest extending from the northeast to southwest and "resting" on the pleasant mountain valleys of Štavna and Carina (1800-1900m of altitude). Unlike Durmitor (18 km), due to its limited length (7 km) Kom is more lucid. It certainly doesn` t lack either in craggy gorges, inaccessible pyramids or crumbling terrains that on a stormy weatherin the spring fall into the valley like the `stony river`. Watched from distance Kom reminds on some kind of a cap but if you get closer you` ll see its peaks coming in sight. There has been a discussion if there are two or three main peaks of the Kom. According to Rovinski, there are 3 peaks, of which two belong to Kučki Kom and the other to Vasojevićki Kom.

A word `kom` can be derived from an Albanian word `komp` that stands for mountain range, crest or knot, a knot where from mountains extend along which waters flow in the in the spring fall into the valley like the `stony river`. Watched from distance Kom reminds on some kind of a cap but if you get closer you` ll see its peaks coming in sight. There has been a discussion if there are two or three main peaks of the Kom. According to Rovinski, there are 3 peaks, of which two belong to Kučki Kom and the other to Vasojevićki Kom. A word `kom`

Bjelasica   Bjelasica

Visitorsko jezero

Trnovačko Lake is situated in the middle of the ountain range of Volujak, Maglic and Bioc. The lake has the form of the heart and it is placed at an altitude of 1517m and with the surface of 399.250m^2 with the biggest depth of 9,2 m.

Kom represents the key point where from valleys and sprouts are reflecting like the first morning sunshines. The Komovi - this is the place where from rivers start their flow.

Žijevo - 2184m

Mrtvica Canyon

Rikavačko Lake is situated at the foot of Žijevo Mountain at an altitude of 1311m. Its surface is 117.755m² and its depth is 13,9m.

Bukumirsko Lake is situated at the north foot of Žijevo Mountain at an altitude of 1440m. Its surface is 19.320m² and depth is 16,8m. It is the deepest mountain lake of Montenegro after Black Lake.

According to the legend the lake got its name after the folk or tribe called Bukumiri that disappeared because of the internal struggles. A word `Bukumir` means `good bread` in English, which is a complete paradox concerning belligerency and destiny of the tribe.

Piva

Skakavica

Tara River is called "The Tear of Europe" as it has been proclaimed the cleanest river in Europe according to the experts' analysis.

Durmitor

can be derived from an Albanian word `komp` that stands for mountain range, crest or knot, a knot where from mountains extend along which waters flow in theway the herds jump and break the fences at the beginning of autumn.

Kom is located in the most beautiful part of Montenegro.

Special attraction for tourist is rafting down the capricious, turbulent rapids of the perfectly clear Tara to the large calm but more powerful the Drina River. The Tara River and Piva River form the Drina River at the place near the village of Šćepan Polje. A historical development of this area is described in many books of Ivo Andrić, a Nobel Prize winner who had a winter house in Herceg Novi, Montenegro.

The Piva Canyon is enclosed at Plužine by dam of 220m, that is the highest object of that kind in Europe with an accumulative lake of 45 km and useful reservoir volume of 800 million m^3.

"The impossible things could happen here - a man had "moved" ramparts of the monastery (the Monastery of Piva founded between 1573-1583) and its frescoes, enclosed and bridged the canyon, made capricious river calm and turned it into lake".

In this unique nature beauty of the zone of the highest mountain of Montenegro, Durmitor (the peak of Bobotov kuk of 2522m), mountain towns of Žabljak, Šavnik and Plužine are placed.

Šavnik (570 resident) is situated on 840m altitude, on tre half way between Nikšić and Žabljak.

In terms of tourism, the most important of them is Žabljak. It`s the coldest town in the territory of former Yugoslavia (+15°C in July, -4°C in January) with average precipitation, mostly confined to snow of 1450 mm.

Plužine (1494 residents) is situated on the southwestern part of the artificial Mratinjsko Lake. Pivski monastery dating from 1573 is situated nerby Pluzine.

In terms of tourism, the most important of them is Žabljak. It`s the coldest town in the territory of former Yugoslavia (+15°C in July, -4°C in January) with average precipitation, mostly confined to snow of 1450 mm. This makes it one of the most interesting destinations for winter sport and for development of winter tourism in general, while its fresh and clean air makes it also visited during the summer season.

Nikšić is 2065 km^2 large and is one of the largest townships in the Balkans. Under the

Nevidio canyon - detail

Plužine - panorama

Pivsko lake - detail
In 1975, a dam of 220m was built on the Tara River and Pivsko Lake was formed in that way. Pivsko Lake is 42m long and it is up to 1 km wide. The length of the dam arch at its top is 261m and the maximal dam width is 40m.

The most important cultural historic monument is Piva Monastery. Its construction started in 1573 and lasted to 1586. Herzegovian metropolitan, later the patriarch of Peć, Savatije, erected it. Piva Monastery possesses fabulously rich treasury and it represented the most important spiritual and cultural centre of this area over the centuries.
Piva Monastery (1573-86) was "moved" together with its wall decoration (1260m²) from the spring of the Piva, stone by stone, because of the construction of the hydro water plant, which represents the greatest conservatory undertaking of that kind. It is situated 9 km away from the town of Plužine. The process of "moving" of the Piva Monastery lasted from 1970-1982.

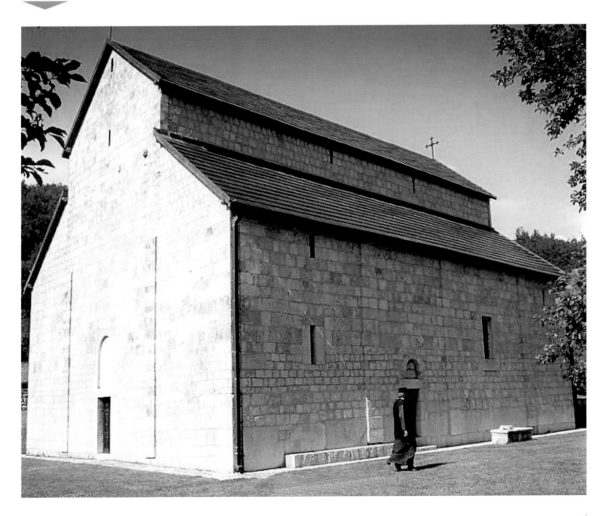

Nikšić

Although it is 60 kilometers away from the sea while Cetinje is only 13, Nikšić is thanks to the valley of Zeta and Bjelopavlići warmer than Cetinje.

Zeta River is a lost river and it is the largest tributary of the Morača River. The springs of Vidrovan and Vuk`s fountainheads in Nikšićko Field form the Zeta River, where from it flows 21 km long to the Head of the Zeta where it has its headwaters and where, after 50 km, it empties into the Morača.

Škrčko lake

The Tara Canyon *is, due to its 1300m high sides, the deepest in Europe and second in the world, after the Colorado Canyon in the USA.*

Durmitor- Ševarita lokva

Pljevlja - Holy Trinity Monastery was first mentioned in 1537. Its construction was started by a hieromonk Visarion and his brother Sava and finally ended thanks to the efforts of monk Georgije. Its present-day appearance it got in 1875/76.

Hussein-Pasha Mosque with a minaret of 42m high was erected in 1562. It was built according to the model of Mehmed Pasha Sokolović' s "medresa" in Istanbul ("medresa"- a Muslim religious secondary school). The Koran from the 16th century is kept in this mosque.

Bijelo Polje

Plavsko Lake is situated at an altitude of 907 m and it is the largest mountain lake in Montenegro. Its space during the dry period is 2 square kilometers, and its biggest depth is 9,15 m. Lim River flows out of it.

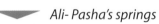 Prokletije

Ali- Pasha's springs

name of Nikšić it was first mentioned in one document from Dubrovnik in 1355. This place had always been exposed to different conquerors, the Turks, the Austro-Hungarians and others. Today, Nikšić is the industrial centre of Montenegro.

Nikšić was first known as Anagastum, then as Onogošt and nowadays as Nikšić after the tribe of Nikšići. The Church of St. Vasilije of Ostrog and King Nicola's Palace are situated on the small hill in the centre of the town. King Nicola erected the church to commemorate the death of the Montenegrins and Herzegovians killed in the liberation wars against the Turks, 1875-1878.

The ramparts of the ancient town of **Andrijevica** Onogošt date from the 4th century. It was erected on the foundations of the Roman camp, then in the Middle Age, it became one of the Serbian towns and later a Turkish fortress.

The town of **Pljevlja** was first mentioned in 1469. It can be said that it lies on coal - lignite. Two medieval religious monuments of Pljevlja, Monastery of Holy Trinity erected in 1537 and Husein - Pasha`s Mosque from 1562 represent the pride of this town.

The municipality of Pljevlja is the ancient settlement dating from the Bronze Age. The oldest monuments are tumuli dating from 1500 BC. According to Turkish register from 1908, the population of Pljevlja was 14000 inhabitants. Like Nikšić, Pljevlja also represents the industrial town (steam power plant, coal mines, cement factory, timber company...). Different monuments of material and spiritual

Church of St. Ilija in Komovi mountain, near Podgorica, was built on 1800 m above sea-level. Only few temples in Europe are built so high.

culture make this town more interesting. A tourist will experience an authentic national ornament as soon as he encounters `stećaci` (old Bosnian tombstones), Orthodox monasteries and mosques with arabesques decoration.

The highest mountains in Montenegro are Prokletije (Maja Voljat 2694m), Durmitor (Bobotov Kuk 2523 m), Komovi (Kom Kucki 2487 m),Volujak (Volujak 2336 m), Sinjajevina (Babin zub 2277 m). The highest mountain peak in Montenegro is Maja Voljat in Prokletije, 2694 m, than Bobotov Kuk, 2523 m.

THE VALLEY OF LIM RIVER

The highway leads to the town of Berane and at the town of Rožaje it leaves Montenegro. The remains of the ancient civilizations from the Neolithic, the Roman Time and medieval Serbian culture are kept in the town of Berane. After the building of the Monastery Đurđevi Stupovi at the end of the 12th century, it became the centre of Serbian Bishopric in 1219.

During the summer and winter season, people attracted with its recreation areas, of which mountain Jalovica is the most famous, and with the restaurants famous for its local specialties come to take a rest and enjoy this lovely place (dairy products, river trout, mountain lamb, plum brandy, well-known `dapsićke` apples...).

Andrijevica is a small mountain town located on the highway to Plav and via Čakor, the road curve at the highest altitude in the former Yugoslavia (1849m) to Peć (Kosovo). The settlement is of low-road type with interesting houses made of stone and wood (ground floor called `izba` is made of stone while first floor and roof are wooden).

Plav is a town situated on Plavsko Lake, at the spring of the Lim River. The valley of Plav is surrounded with high mountains of the Visitor and Prokletije. The Prokletije are the rockiest mountains in the Balkans. According to Yugoslav geo-morphologist Jovan Cvijić " they make the imposing impression and because of the wilderness they inspire anxiety and fear". This area is particularly attractive to

hunters due to the richness in game animals- roe deer, chamois, bears, boars, partridges, grouse.

The town of **Gusinje** is situated in the high mountain region of the Prokletije at 939m above sea level. It was first mentioned in the 14th century. The area of the town of Bijelo Polje and the part of Sanjak was under the Turkish dominance until the First Balkan War in 1912. That period of history greatly influenced this region and it is best visible in its oriental coloured religion and folklore. In direct vicinity of the town, there are springs of mineral waters of balneo-therapeutic importance.

Biogradska gora

SKI CENTRES

Žabljak, a small town situated in the middle of the National Park "Durmitor" at an altitude of 1453m is one of the leading winter centres of Montenegro. Intact and luxury nature with abundance of pure white snow, diverse evergreen trees and lovely landscapes is adapted to visitors, nature lovers and to those who like skiing in particular.

There are three ski centres on Žabljak: "Savin kuk", "Bosača" and "Jovorača". The most famous of them is "Savin kuk" that can meet the expectations of even more demanding skiers. Ski run is 3,5 km long with the capacity of 4,000 skiers per hour. This ski centre also has two cableways, a ski lift and two baby ski lifts. It is equipped for night skiing, with ski services and ski schools. As inevitable part of this attractive destination are different tourist objects.

Ski centre "Jovorovača" has a ski run of 400m long, a baby ski lift and a ski school. On Žabljak`s ski runs you will enjoy motor sledge driving, riding a horse, driving horse-drawn sledge or taking up some of winter sports, Nordic skiing or walking along the marked paths.

Kolašin - This winter centre is situated between central and northern part of Montenegro at an altitude of 950m, at the foot of the mountain massifs of Komovi, Bjelasica and Sinjajevina, just next to the National Park "Biogradska Gora". Beside its ideal altitude and favourable climate for winter sports, Kolašin also has an ideal geographic position. It is situated on a highway Beograd -

Durmitor

121

Bar, only 80 km away from Podgorica.

Railway link Bar-Beograd also passes through Kolašin, which makes it possible to get from this place to Montenegrin coast in only 90 minutes. Skijalište „Jezerine" nalazi se na 1420 m nadmorske visine, a od grada je udaljeno 8,5 km.

Ski centre "Jezerine" is situated at an altitude of 1420 m and it is 8,5 km away from the town.

Ski centre is equipped with two-seat ski lift of 1800m long, a capacity of 1200 skiers per hour, three ski lifts of 500m and a baby ski lift of 150m. Total length of the ski run is 15 km, a capacity of 8000 skiers at the same time.

There are several ski schools, ski services as well as following tourist objects.

A winter sport- **recreational centre "Lokve"** is situated 15 km away from Berane. It is located at an altitude of 1335-1675m. There are a two-seat cableway with two ski lifts and a capacity of 1000 skiers per hour. Ski run is 5 km long. Ski centre "Lokve" is situated on mountain of Smiljevica.

Rožaje - Ski centre "Turjak"

In the utmost northeast part of Montenegro, near the Ibar River, the town of Rožaje is situated. Rožaje is one of the ski centres of Montenegro. On a way to Berane, 4 km away from the town a ski centre "Turjak" is placed.

This ski centre has grown into important and modern ski destination of Montenegro. Ski

Durmitor

centre is equipped with two ski lifts of 2,3 km long, a capacity of 2000 skiers, a ski school and a ski service.

Ski centre "Turjak" can satisfy the most demanding fans of snow and winter skills. There are two baby lifts near the motel "Bogaje".

Nikšić-Ski centre "Vučje"

Tourist-recreational centre "Vučje" is 20 km away from Nikšić on a highway to Žabljak. There are four ski runs: one recreational, two for competitions and one for the youngest. Ski centre is equipped with three ski lifts, a ski service and a ski school.

There are also several smaller ski centres in Montenegro, such as "Kosanica", "Veruša" and "Ivanova korita".

- Ski centre "Kosanica" is located on the mountain of Ljubišnja" in the vicinity of Pljevlja. It is of local character and mostly visited by people of Pljevlja and nearby places.

- Ski centre "Veruša" is a small ski centre at the foot of Komovi, 50 km away from Podgorica. It is, mostly, favourite recreation area of school children. There are two baby ski lifts and a children resort in the direct vicinity.

- Ski centre "Ivanova korita" is 14 km away from Cetinje.

Airports

There are two international airports, in Podgorica and Tivat.

Airport "Golubovci" (Podgorica) is 12 km away from Podgorica, 80 km away from Kolašin, 62 km away from Budva and 50 km away from Bar.

Airport "Tivat" is 3 km away from Tivat, 4 km away from Kotor, 60 km away from Bar and 84 km away from Ulcinj.

THINGS TO DO IN MONTENEGRO

Rafting

Snow kite surfing

Mountaineering

Diving

Ballooning

Fishing

Water kite surfing

Food

Food in Montenegro is diverse and it depends on a place you are. The coastal food is rich in fish, olives and cereals while the continental is based on dairy products, "red" meat and potato.

CONTENT

PUBLISHER

Mapa Crne Gore

tel. 069/ 676-603

FOR THE PUBLISHER

Vladimir Mijović

EDITOR

Milun Lutovac

PHOTOS

Arhiv MTC

Arhiv turističke organizacije Crne Gore

Branislav Strugar

Arhiv Mape Crne Gore

Foto Papić

Isidor Stankov

DESIGN

Mijović Vladimir

Mirjana Radovanović

Jovana Lukač

PREPRESS, CTP AND PRESS

Golbi print - Podgorica

PRESS RUN

2000 kom

CIP - Каталогизација у публикацији
Народна библиотека Србије, Београд

338.48(497.16)(036)

CRNA GORA / [urednik Mijović Vladimir ; autor teksta
Milun Lutovac]. - Beograd : Mapa Crne Gore, 2007 (Beograd : Skener Studio Lazić). - 120 str. : fotogr. ; 30 cm

Podatak o autoru uzet iz kolofona. - Tiraž 2.000.

ISBN 978-86-84543-25-9

1. Мијовић, Владимир
a) Туризам - Црна Гора - Водичи
COBISS.SR-ID 139468300